PICTURE LIBRARY

DOGS

PICTURE LIBRARY
DOGS

Norman Barrett

Franklin Watts

London New York Sydney Toronto

© 1990 Franklin Watts

Franklin Watts Inc
387 Park Avenue South
New York
NY 10016

Printed in Italy

Designed by
Barrett & Weintroub

Photographs by
Marc Henrie
Metropolitan Police
N.S. Barrett Collection
Guide Dogs for the Blind Association
R.P. Oldham

Illustration by
Rhoda & Robert Burns

Technical Consultant
Rhoda Burns

Library of Congress Cataloging-in-Publication Data

Barrett, Norman S.
    Dogs/Norman Barrett.
        p.   cm. — (Picture library)
    Summary: Describes different types of dogs, their behavior, life
cycle, and roles in domestic and wild environments.
        ISBN 0-531-14040-7
    1. Dogs—Juvenile literature. [1. Dogs.] I. Title.
II. Series.
SF426.5.B38   1990
636.7—dc20
                                                                89-29346
                                                                    CIP
                                                                    AC

APR   '91

Contents

Introduction

Dogs are popular pets, and many also do important work. Some breeds (kinds) make excellent guide dogs for the blind. Others are used to help herd livestock. There are also watchdogs and dogs that help the police with their work.

Of all the animals, dogs have the greatest range of appearance. There are big ones and small ones, dogs with shaggy coats and dogs with smooth coats, and they come in a wide variety of colors.

△ A Deerhound greets a tiny Dachshund puppy. They might look very different, but they are both dogs. In fact, they both belong to the same group of dogs — hounds.

If brought up correctly, dogs make loyal and affectionate companions. They are intelligent and obedient animals, and most kinds are playful.

Dogs have a highly developed sense of smell and excellent hearing. They show their feelings not only by barking, howling and growling, but by the way they carry their tail and with other body signals.

△ Three pets pose proudly for the photographer in the park. With good training, dogs make obedient pets and get along well together when they meet. These are, from left to right, a Golden Retriever, a Chinese Crested and a Cavalier King Charles Spaniel.

Looking at dogs

There are more varieties of dog than there are of any other animal. The hundreds of breeds of dogs range from the tiny Chihuahua, no bigger than a man's hand, to the Irish Wolfhound, which can stand on its hind legs and rest its paws on a person's shoulders.

Golden Retriever

Miniature Poodle

Wire-Haired Fox Terrier

Chihuahua

Cavalier King Charles Spaniel

Border Collie

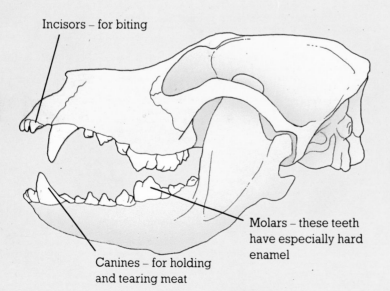

Incisors – for biting

Canines – for holding and tearing meat

Molars – these teeth have especially hard enamel

A dog's skull

A dog's jaws and teeth are very large and powerful in relation to the rest of the skull. The dog cannot move its lower jaw sideways. This is why dogs seem to tear and gulp at their food rather than chewing it as we do. The flat back teeth (molars) are used for gnawing and crushing.

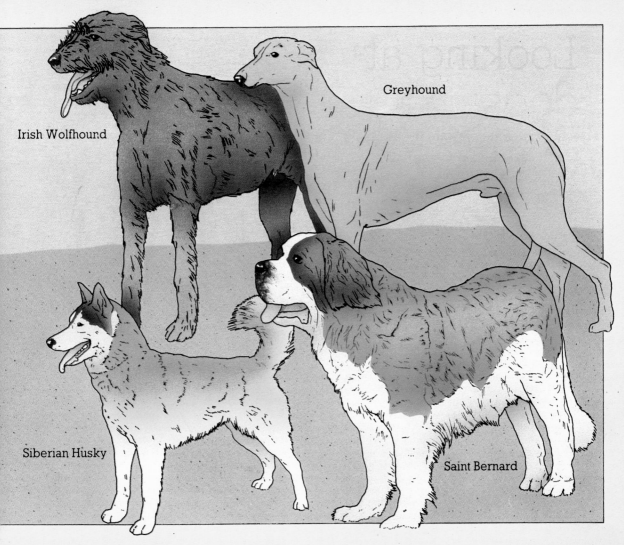

Irish Wolfhound

Greyhound

Siberian Husky

Saint Bernard

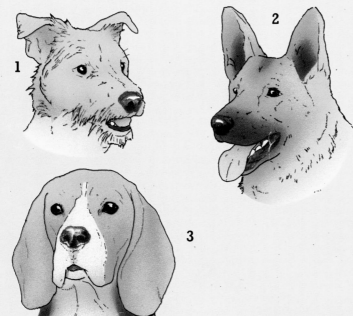

1

2

3

Ears

Dogs' ears vary enormously in size and shape. Some terriers, for example, have tulip ears (1), the German Shepherd has prick ears (2) and the Beagle has floppy ears (3). Other types of ears include bat ears (Corgi), blunt-tipped, erect ears (Chow Chow), flat drop ears (Poodle) and rose ears (Whippet). All puppies' ears are small and closed at birth. In some breeds, it is several months before they take on their final shape.

Behavior

Many of the things that dogs do are inherited from their wild ancestors, such as wolves and coyotes. They regard their owner's house as their territory, with themselves as part of the family, their "pack."

Strange dogs may be threatening or friendly, shy or even frightened. A well trained dog will not bite unless it is trained to attack intruders. Beware a dog that snarls and stares, with a stiff posture and its tail held high.

▽ Dogs enjoy playing around, especially when they are young. They have plenty of energy and can play noisily with each other if left by themselves, without becoming aggressive.

△ Training a dog to
obey orders and
signals. When training a
dog, it is important to be
firm if they do wrong,
and to praise good
behavior.

▷ When two dogs
meet, they first sniff
nose to nose, and then
smell each other's
bodies all over.

▷ Often when two dogs meet, one will be dominant over the other. This will not necessarily depend on the size of the dogs. A dog showing submission might lie down and roll onto its back.

▽ Dogs enjoy playing in water, and never seem to get tired of retrieving sticks or toys.

Birth and growing up

Female dogs carry their young for about 9 weeks before they are born. They have litters of from 1 to as many as 12 or more puppies.

A female nurses her pups for about 6 weeks after they are born. The best time to take a puppy as a pet is at 8 weeks.

Dogs become fully grown between about 8 months and 2 years. They live for about 12 to 15 years, although larger dogs generally have a shorter life span.

▽ A mother nurses her three puppies. They feed on their mother's milk for the first 4 to 5 weeks.

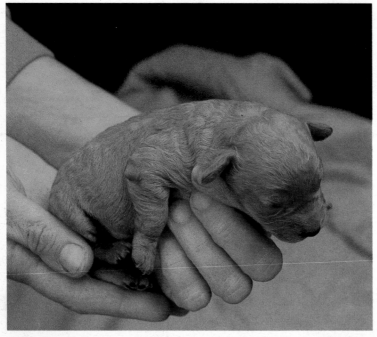

◁ A week-old puppy. Puppies are born with their ears and eyes closed.

▷ An Irish Setter with her litter. Mothers are very protective of their young.

▽ It's too late to reprimand puppies after they have misbehaved. They should be spoken to firmly when caught in the act!

Kinds of dogs

Different kinds of dogs have been bred over thousands of years. A purebred dog has parents from the same breed. Mongrels are dogs from parents of mixed breeds. If two dogs of different breeds mate, their offspring may be called cross-breeds.

Dog breeding organizations, often known as kennel clubs, set standards for each breed. They also classify breeds in groups, such as working dogs, terriers or toy dogs.

▽ Two non-pedigree dogs, or mongrels. The majority of dogs in the world are mongrels.

△ The Shetland
Sheepdog belongs to
the working group. It is
a gentle, sweet-natured
dog with a beautiful
coat. It is always eager
to please and is known
for its loyalty.

▷ The Bichon Frise is a
member of the toy
group. Toy dogs are
bred as pets, and
especially to look sweet
and appealing. Bichon
is French for lapdog
and frise means curly,
referring to the coat.

17

◁ Bassett Hounds are gentle and devoted pets. But although they are calm and may appear lazy, they are hunting dogs, and need lots of exercise.

▽ The Dalmatian is one of the best known breeds of dog because of its spots. It is classified in the utility, or non-sporting, group, and makes a fine guard dog.

△ This is a cross between a Bearded and a Border Collie. Collies are sheepdogs. They are very loyal and make excellent watchdogs.

▷ This beautifully bred and groomed Afghan Hound has the bearing of a champion. Afghans can be of any of several colors and are notable for their long, silky coat. They are fast runners and make lively pets. They enjoy affection, but are not as eager to please as some dogs.

△ The Cocker Spaniel, slightly smaller than the English Cocker, is a very popular pet in the United States. It belongs to the sporting group, and still has all of its hunting instincts.

◁ A Shih Tzu with its puppy. The Shih Tzu is a toy dog that originated in ancient China. It has a small, bewhiskered face with a long beard and a trailing coat. The adult can look just as cute as the puppy.

▷ The Rottweiler has a reputation for being a very fierce dog. It is used as a guard dog and can be trained to attack intruders. It will not stand for too much handling by strangers, but a properly trained Rottweiler should not be vicious.

▽ A smooth-haired Dachshund. Dachshunds have long, low bodies, shaped to go down holes in search of small animals.

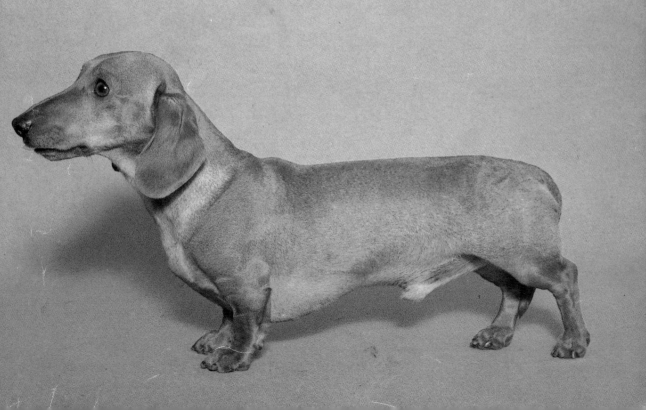

Terriers make up a large group of dogs with varying appearance. They make excellent watchdogs and kill pests such as rats. They were originally bred for driving game out of holes, and their name comes from "terra," the Latin word for earth.

◁ Smooth-haired Fox Terriers.

▽ The Kerry Blue Terrier.

Working dogs of today

Dogs help people in many ways. Police dogs are specially trained for tracking criminals, as guard dogs and for other types of work. German Shepherds, Doberman Pinschers and Airedale Terriers make good police dogs.

Other uses for dogs include herding animals, pulling sleds, search and rescue work and helping blind or deaf people.

△ German Shepherd dogs, or Alsatians, being trained for police work take little notice of a cat that happens to be passing by. Intelligent animals with highly developed senses, Shepherds also make good sheepdogs, guide dogs for the blind and family companions.

△ The Border Collie is an excellent working sheepdog. Collies enjoy their work, controlling and guarding flocks of sheep, and have boundless energy and stamina.

◁ A spaniel working for a security police force checks for explosives. These "sniffer" dogs are used at airports and other places to combat terrorism and drug smuggling.

Several types of dog have been trained to help people in trouble or who are handicapped in some way.

Some large dogs are bred for rescue work. The Newfoundland loves water, and has a fine record for saving people from drowning. Saint Bernards and German Shepherds are expert mountain rescue dogs.

German Shepherds are also trained as guide dogs for the blind, along with Labradors, Golden Retrievers and some other breeds.

▽ Training for a Newfoundland rescue dog includes towing a boat. These gentle animals are excellent swimmers, and learn to tow a victim by an arm.

◁ A guide dog steers its master around an unexpected obstacle on the pavement. Guide dogs serve as the "eyes" of blind people.

▽ Gundogs are used for retrieving game birds when they have been shot down.

Wild dogs

Dogs belong to a family that also includes wild animals such as wolves, coyotes and jackals.

Wild dogs include the hunting dogs of Africa and the dholes of southern Asia. Like wolves, these wild dogs hunt in packs.

The bush dogs of South America can be tamed. They are often kept as pets by Amazon Indians. The dingoes of Australia are thought to be domestic dogs that have returned to the wild.

△ The wolf is the largest member of the dog family, although certain breeds of domestic dogs, such as the Irish Wolfhound and the Saint Bernard, might be slightly taller or heavier.

The story of dogs

The first pet

Dogs were the first animals to be domesticated, about 12,000 years ago or even earlier. The people of those times moved about, hunting animals and gathering plants. Packs of scavenging wild dogs probably followed these wandering tribes, feeding on scraps of food left behind.

As wild dogs began to depend on people for food, the people realized the value of dogs. They kept the campsite clean by eating the waste matter, and their barking warned of danger from animals such as bears. People began to tame dogs, and they probably also reared them from puppies.

Hunters found dogs useful in picking up the scent of wild animals, and this encouraged the domestication of dogs. Civilized peoples, too, used dogs for hunting. They developed special breeds of dogs for hunting and for herding sheep. The ancient Romans also kept dogs as pets.

△ One of the world's best-known dogs, a Fox Terrier called Nipper, shown listening to an early gramophone in a painting by Francis Barraud. This became famous as the trademark for the record company Victor Talking Machine/RCA, and appeared on millions of record labels.

△ Carvings more than 2,500 years old on the walls of an ancient Assyrian palace show dogs being used in combat.

Breeding

Breeding dogs began in early times. If special features or abilities were required, dogs strong in these characteristics were mated. For example, size could be developed in this way, and large dogs were bred for hunting or fighting. Fast dogs were bred for hunting speedy prey.

Thousands of years ago in

southwestern Asia, mastiff-type dogs were developed and these large animals were used in battle and to hunt lions and guard temples. Greyhounds were bred for hunting gazelle.

△ An Afghan Hound being judged for obedience in a dog show.

Dog shows and kennel clubs

Dogs became much-loved companions to people in most civilizations, both as working animals and as pets. Most of today's breeds were developed by the 1800s. Standards for various breeds were set up and the first dog shows took place. Societies called kennel clubs were founded to regulate breeds.

Overbreeding

Dog breeders have been criticized for going too far sometimes in developing certain features. In their efforts to perfect a particular quality, they might also introduce defects into a breed. A good example of such overbreeding is the Bulldog. The exaggerated flatness of its face has affected its breathing, and it also suffers heart attacks.

△ Bulldogs in a painting of over 100 years ago. Here they are showing the first signs of a flattened muzzle, but their nose is lower than their eyes and their jaw only slightly upturned.

△ The Bulldog of today has a very flattened muzzle, with its jaw turned right up so that its nose is about level with its eyes. It has a stockier appearance, with a larger head and shorter legs.

Facts and records

Size

The smallest dog is the Chihuahua. Healthy specimens of this Mexican breed of toy dogs may stand only 13 cm (5 in) at the shoulders, and weigh as little as 1 kg (2 lb).

The tallest breed is the Irish Wolfhound, standing as high as 98 cm (38 in) at the shoulders. The Saint Bernard is the heaviest breed, weighing as much as 100 kg (220 lb) or more.

△ Four generations of Boxers — puppies with their mother (right), grandfather (left) and great-grandmother (center).

△ The Chihuahua is the smallest breed.

Ageing

Dogs develop more quickly than humans and have much shorter lives. A 6-month-old puppy may be compared with a 10-year-old child in development, and a 2-year-old dog is about equivalent to a 24-year-old person. After that, each year of a dog's life is roughly equal to 4 or 5 years of a person's life.

Dogs rarely live more than 20 years, although the greatest age recorded is over 29.

△ The Chow Chow is the only breed of dog with a blue-black tongue.

Glossary

Breed
A recognized type of dog. The standards for a particular breed may vary from country to country, and not all breeds are recognized worldwide.

Crossbreed
A dog bred from parents of two different purebred dogs.

Dog show
An event in which various breeds of dog are judged and rated according to how they meet the standards set for a particular breed. Prizes are awarded to the best dogs in each breed and the best dog overall. Tests for agility and obedience are usually held as separate events.

Groups
Kennel clubs classify the various breeds in groups, such as hounds or working dogs, mainly for the purpose of organizing dog shows. Groups vary slightly from country to country.

Kennel club
The organization that sets the standards for each breed, recognizes new breeds, registers purebred dogs, and supervises shows.

Litter
All the puppies born at one time to the same mother.

Mongrel
A dog whose parents are from mixed breeds. Sometimes called a "mutt."

Muzzle
The projecting part of an animal's face, the jaws and nose.

Non-pedigree dog
A dog not recognized as being purebred. Mongrels and cross-breeds are non-pedigrees.

Purebred
A dog whose parents belong to the same breed.

Utility
A group of breeds, for show purposes, that do not fit into the other groups of breeds; also called the non-sporting group.

Working dogs
A group of breeds for show purposes, but a term that may also be applied to any dog that performs work for people.

Index